Where Did Math Symbols Come From?

By Veda Boyd Jones

CELEBRATION PRESS
Pearson Learning Group

Contents

What Is a Symbol?

A **symbol** is a picture or object that stands for something else. A flag is a symbol. It can stand for a country. The letters of the alphabet are symbols that stand for sounds. A heart is a symbol for love.

Symbols also help you to do math. Math symbols help you to count and to keep track of things. Math symbols also tell you what to do to solve a math problem. Read on to learn more about some math symbols.

An American flag is a symbol for the United States of America.

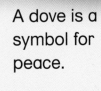

A dove is a symbol for peace.

Numbers

Numbers are symbols that stand for a certain amount. The number symbols you use developed from symbols used in India more than two thousand years ago. These ancient number symbols were used to keep records of goods that were traded.

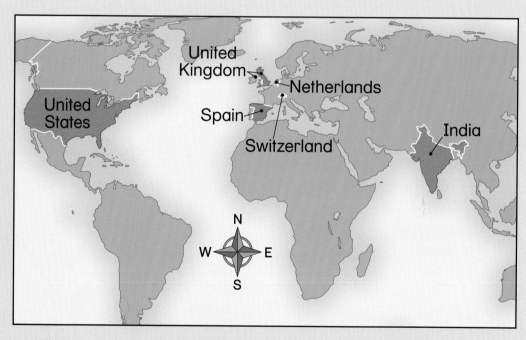

This map shows the different areas in the world where the math symbols discussed in this book came from.

Different Number Symbols

Not all people use the same number symbols. Here are some symbols developed in different countries:

United States	Ancient Greece	China
1	α	一
2	β	二
3	γ	三
4	δ	四
5	ε	五

At first, the number symbols used in India did not include a symbol for zero. Zero is a symbol that stands for no things. Other ancient people did not use a symbol for zero either. Several hundred years after they created the first number symbols, the ancient Indians invented a symbol for zero. They were the first people to do so.

Plus Sign and Minus Sign

You probably know the **plus sign** (+) and **minus sign** (–). A plus sign in a math problem means to add. A minus sign in a math problem means to subtract. But did you know that these symbols didn't always stand for addition or subtraction?

In math, symbols tell you how to solve the problem.

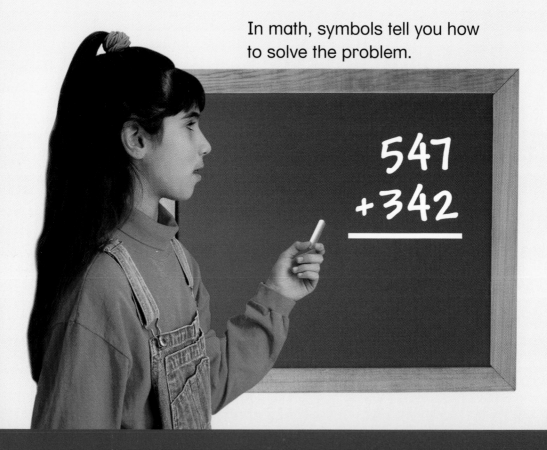

547
+342

Long ago, merchants in Europe sold things in sacks or barrels. If a sack was too full, they marked it with a + symbol. If it was not full, they marked it with a − symbol. Back then, the + symbol stood for "too much" and the − symbol stood for "not enough."

In the early 1500s, a **mathematician** in the Netherlands used these signs to show addition and subtraction in math problems. By the mid-1500s, the signs were used in an English math book.

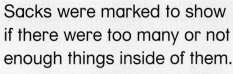

Sacks were marked to show if there were too many or not enough things inside of them.

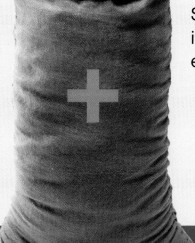

Equal Sign

Another math symbol you might know is the **equal sign** (=). In a math problem, the equal sign means that one thing has the same amount as another. It is an easy way of showing that two things are the same. However, many years ago, showing that two things were equal was not very easy.

$$12 + 10 = 22$$

$$43 + 12 = 55$$

$$28 - 16 = 12$$

$$30 - 15 = 15$$

The equal sign shows that the numbers on the left side are equal to the numbers on the right side.

Hundreds of years ago, if people wanted to show 2 + 2 = 4, they would write "2 + 2 is equal to 4." However, around 500 years ago, a mathematician from Wales, part of the United Kingdom, decided that using words was too much trouble. So he invented the equal sign. That equal sign is the same symbol that is used today.

ATLANTIC OCEAN

Scotland

Northern Ireland

Ireland

England

Wales

Equal Lines

Robert Recorde was the mathematician who invented the equal sign. He introduced the sign in a math book he wrote in 1557. He drew the sign to look like two lines that were exactly the same distance apart. Lines described that way are called parallel lines.

Multiplication Sign

The **multiplication sign** (x) in a math problem is a fast way of showing that a number should be added to itself a certain number of times. For example, 5 x 3 means that 5 should be added to itself 3 times. About 400 years ago, an English mathematician used this symbol to show multiplication.

At the time, the x symbol was already used to show another math idea. Other symbols were used to show multiplication. Then, about 150 years ago, the x symbol was used to teach multiplication in math textbooks.

In 1628, William Oughtred, an English mathematician, used the x sign as a symbol for multiplication in a book that he wrote.

Multiplication Symbols

Other symbols can be used to show multiplication. Here are some different symbols used in multiplication problems:

5 ⨯ 4 = 20
5 ∗ 4 = 20
5 · 4 = 20

Division Sign

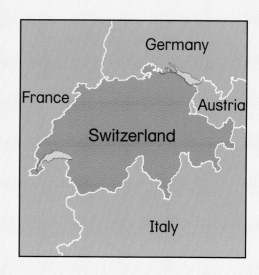

The **division sign** (÷) tells you to divide things or to group them into equal amounts. Hundreds of years ago, this sign was actually used to show subtraction! Then, about 350 years ago, a mathematician from Switzerland used the symbol to show division. About ten years later, an English math book also used the symbol for division. People stopped using the symbol for subtraction and started using it for division.

$$8 \div 4 = 2$$

$$9 \div 3 = 3$$

The division sign in a math problem tells you to put things into equal groups.

Greater Than Sign and Less Than Sign

The **greater than sign** and **less than sign** show numbers that are not equal. The greater than symbol (>) shows that the number to its left is greater than the number to its right. The less than symbol (<) shows that the number to its left is less than the number to its right. Both symbols were first used in a math book written about 400 years ago in England.

Other Greater Than and Less Than Symbols

Other symbols have been used to show unequal things. Compare the symbols we use today to symbols used long ago.

Symbol Name	Symbol Used Today	Symbol Used Long Ago
greater than	>	⊐
less than	<	⊏

Cent Sign and Dollar Sign

You may know the symbols that are used to show money. The cent sign (¢) shows money that is less than one dollar. A short line is printed through the letter *c* to show that it is a money symbol and not a letter of the alphabet. This symbol was first used about 200 years ago.

The dollar sign ($) became an American money symbol more than 200 years ago when the United States was a new country. Before that time, the dollar sign was actually used to show Spanish money.

$1.00 each

The dollar sign and cent sign were invented to show money.

LEMONADE 25¢

Doing math is easier and faster when you use math symbols. Imagine if there were no math symbols. Instead of using the multiplication sign x, you would have to write out the words *multiplied by* every time you worked on a multiplication problem. The names of numbers would have to be written, too. Instead of writing 100, you would have to write the words *one hundred*. You can understand why math symbols are important.

Glossary

division sign (÷) math symbol for division

equal sign (=) math symbol that shows that one thing has the same amount as another

greater than sign (>) math symbol that shows that a number is greater than another number

less than sign (<) math symbol that shows that a number is less than another number

mathematician person who is an expert in math

minus sign (–) math symbol for subtraction

multiplication sign (x) math symbol for multiplication

plus sign (+) math symbol for addition

symbol a picture or object that stands for something else

Index